THE 100 BEST
INTERIORS & HOUSES IN WOOD

BETA-PLUS

THE 100 BEST

INTERIORS & HOUSES IN WOOD

CONTENTS

THE TIMELESS CONTEMPORARY APPEAL
OF A CLASSIC COUNTRY HOUSE

The Costermans company built this classic country house on the leafy outskirts of Antwerp.
A great deal of attention was paid to the choice of materials, such as unusual
antique tiles, old hard-wearing parquet floors and impressive fireplaces. The look is
timeless, and yet contemporary: a sleek and sophisticated living environment.

www.costermans-projecten.be

Home office with a white-lacquered cardboard desk by PB Zone, a Bonacini desk chair and white MDF cupboard units.

Central block with a surface in Portuguese Branco de Mos. A simple cooker hood with wrought-iron surround and a wall in hand-made white Moroccan zeliges.

↖
The living room, with a wengé-tinted oak coffee table by PB Zone and a Linteloo sofa.

TABLEAUX VIVANTS

Architect Olivier Dwek created this apartment for a passionate collector
of contemporary art. The concept is built around her collection.
The large windows open the dialogue with the surrounding
nature: they are real *tableaux vivants*.

www.olivierdwek.com

COASTAL STYLE

This coastside villa was bought and transformed by project developer Hubimmo.
Interior architect Nathalie Van Reeth signed for the interior design.

nathalie.vanreeth@skynet.be   www.hubimmo.com

A COSY HOME IN SOLID WOOD

With seventy-five employees and around seventy projects a year in Belgium and northern France, wood construction company Mi Casa has become a familiar name in the markets for turnkey homes and wood construction. The company has opted to invest in new technology for the entire construction process, in order to remain competitive and to improve quality. They also plan to introduce other modern techniques to upgrade their homes, such as new insulation and ventilation technology.

www.micasa.be

This recent Mi Casa creation is one of the many wooden homes that the company has constructed in New England, America.

↖
A Mi Casa home has a maximum of two floors, plus an attic and a cellar. This type of solid wood structure is a stable house that can cope perfectly with the vertical load of its own weight, the roof and the interior, as well as the horizontal load of the wind.

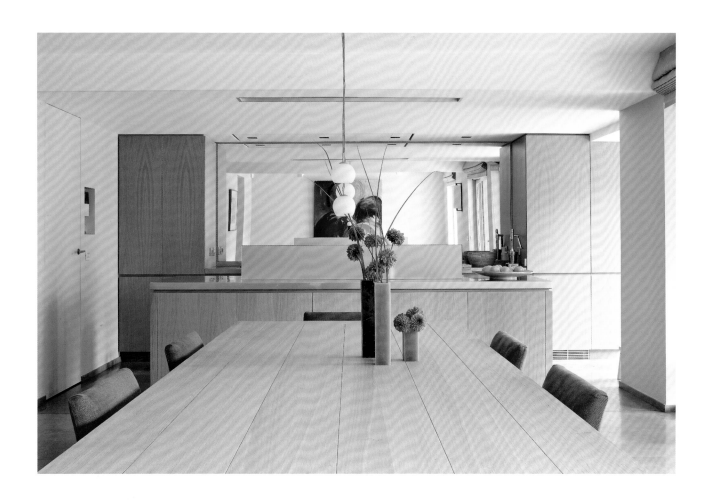

BRIGHT AND COMFORTABLE

A family with four children decided to settle in a semi-detached house in
Brussels and engaged the services of architect Baudouin Courtens.
The dwelling was completely renovated three years ago and is still in very good condition.
However, Courtens understands that the house did not suit this family's way of life.
Consequently, instead of some required interior arrangements, it is a total recasting of
the garden level and the beautiful upper floor that Courtens proposes to his clients.
The result is a bright and comfortable house, a custom-made craft, a reflection
of the modern way of life and the dynamics of the house owner.

www.courtens.be

The living room occupies the whole width of the façade facing the garden. It is structured by horizontal lines from the open chimney and the bench.

↗
On the garden level, all the partitions are removed to create a large open space overlooking the garden, where the kitchen and dining area are located.

↖
The oak and steel kitchen is open yet made intimate by a large sliding panel in front of the central island. A huge mirror that enlarges the space is placed on the wall above the cooking stove.

A discreet air of sobriety, a sober choice of materials and colours. The range is intentionally reduced in order to create a unity in the project.

A CONTEMPORARY TOUCH

Interior designer Nathalie Van Reeth has transformed a
typical semi-detached house dated end of the 19th century
to a both pleasant and contemporary whole.
The objective was to open up the spaces and introduce light into
the house, thus the three rooms that follow one another and the
centre staircase core result in a narrower room in the centre.

nathalie.vanreeth@skynet.be

The wall situated behind the bed forms the structure to the book shelves and lighting partition. The bed is made of tinted oak in the same colour. The bedroom overlooking the dressing room and the bathroom creates an impression of a suite.

↖
The central area is arranged as a library. The ornaments, parquet floor and the old beveled glass door are conserved and carefully restored.

The kitchen is constructed in painted MDF, with the countertop varnished in a darker paint and the floor in whit epoxy. The table is custom-made in wenge tinted wood. The timber floor is painted in the same colour.

The dressing area and the bathroom form a whole. The furniture is finished in the same tinted oak and the old timber floor is painted in a darker colour. Countertops in beige sandstone and tap fitting by Vola.

THE RESTORATION
OF AN 18TH-CENTURY APARTMENT IN BRUSSELS

This apartment is situated on the historic Place des Martyrs,
which has recently been completely restored.
The owners asked Annick Grimmelprez to create a space that would
evoke the eighteenth century in all of its grandeur.
At the same time, the apartment had to fulfil two functions: an exclusive
reception space, and also an atmospheric living environment.

info@annickgrimmelprez.be

Poplar panelling created for a hunting pavilion of Louis XVI (anno 1780, from Stéphane de Harlez). Patina finish by Dankers Decor.
A small kitchenette is concealed behind folding shutters in the panelling (P. van Cronenburg).

THE TIMBERWOOD CONSTRUCTIONS
OF HERITAGE BUILDINGS

Heritage Buildings was the first company to bring oak-framed outbuildings from England to the continent. Now after more than fifteen years they are still indisputably the market leader. Hundreds of pool houses, carports, garages, artists' studios, garden offices, extensions and guest rooms have been built in Belgium and the surrounding countries. Their buildings are as strong and durable as oak, extremely functional and, although designed on traditional lines, often surprisingly modern.

www.heritagebuildings.be

MASTERS OF MODERN ARCHITECTURE

As a specialist in the construction of exclusive villas, Vlassak-Verhulst is not only known for its magnificent country houses and faithful renditions of presbytery-style homes: the company has also earned its spurs in the area of contemporary architecture and interior design. This report about a decidedly contemporary house is a prime example of the mastery that the company displays in this field.

www.vlassakverhulst.com

The floating staircase is a real eye-catcher within the minimalist design of the entrance hall. This staircase is made from brown-black stained oak, with a stainless-steel handrail adding the finishing touch.

A cast-concrete washbasin.

↖
A table in solid oak.
A timber floor in
bleached oak.

QUALITY OF THE HIGHEST STANDARD

Vincent Vangheluwe has been working as a consultant in interior design and the construction sector for fifteen years. Supervising projects at the top of the range (large farmhouses, castles, luxury apartments) has given him a great deal of experience and taught him how to satisfy even the most exacting clients. He works with a team of experienced professionals and coordinates the whole of the construction process: from the structural work to the smallest details of the finish. He will also help the client to select an architect and work on the basis of plans already drawn up by architects.

www.vvtrust.com

The photos in this report were taken in Vincent Vangheluwe's discreet townhouse, in the heart of the Flemish Ardennes.

AN OASIS OF SPACE

As with all of its other projects, the Schellen architectural studio created
both the architecture and the interior of this contemporary home.
Linda Coart was responsible for the functional and clean design,
which extends seamlessly from outside to inside.

www.schellen.be   www.lindacoart.be

The dining room has most contact with the garden because of the beautiful open space with its huge glass section. Curtain frames by Reynaers aluminium ensure a streamlined look. The oak parquet floor has been bleached.

The office at the top of the open space forms a central location with a panoramic view over the beautiful garden.

The Boffi bath with matching basins and fittings is an eye-catching feature in the bathroom.

↖
The long gas fire within the black wall dominates the sitting area. There is also a view of the library and multimedia room from here. The tall wooden sliding door can be used to close off this space.

LIGHT, SPACE, VISION

"Ensemble & Associés": two female interior designers have combined their efforts in this company, following a strict and unique method of working since its inception. They look at the role of light and of details in a new and unusual way, coupling this approach with a thorough knowledge of the client's requirements: every project is carried out in symbiosis with the client's vision. Their hallmark is the idea of complementarity, as is demonstrated by the design of this 300m² home in the heart of the Belgian capital. Light, space, vision: a magic formula with the pure light of fine materials and the lightness of custom-made pieces as a guiding principle. The results of their approach: an exclusive space and a style that is unique.

www.ensembleetassocies.be

A sliding tinted-oak panel provides access to the working area of the library.

The master bathroom. The furniture in the bathroom and the dressing room is made from grey-tinted oak. Floor, walls and surfaces in Grigia Asteria natural stone. The washbasins have been cut into the stone. Mem taps from Dornbracht. Built-in mirrors harmonise with the stone.

THE CHARM OF SOLID WOOD

Unlike the usual wooden skeleton construction, in which a framework of posts and beams is set up, then braced and covered with sheeting material, Mi Casa's solid-wood construction methods involve solid beams joined with tongue-and-groove joints and anchored at all of the corners. The result is a stable structure that can perfectly withstand all of the vertical loads (the weight of the building, the roof, the internal elements), and also the horizontal pressure of the wind. Mi Casa use the dovetail joint in their house construction, a tried-and-tested technique that has proven its value.

www.micasa.be

In this house by Mi Casa, horizontal planks in afrormosia wood and a porch in oak.

AN INVITING PENTHOUSE

This wonderfully located penthouse was designed by Filip Glorieux and his team as the main residence for an active family. The task consisted of connecting three apartments into a single residential whole with different functions that fulfil the wishes of the occupants. Filip Glorieux and his team realised the design, execution and coordination of this unique total project.

www.filipglorieux.be

A central stair connects the bottom apartment (that functions as a reception area and office) and the top apartment with the private accommodation.
An open sense of space is created by using floor to ceiling sliding and turning doors, which allows one optimally to enjoy the breathtaking views.
In their closed position these doors provide the necessary privacy and intimacy.
The restrained colour palette and the careful choice of material ensure a calm whole. Only the magnificent artworks by the occupants provide the necessary frivolity.
This is an apartment in which every member of the family can relax.

↖
Inside and outside form a single whole – this feeling is strengthened by the use of the same materials.
The open fireplace, between kitchen and sitting area, reinforces the open character of this apartment and the cosy atmosphere.

PERFECT HARMONY

With the conversion of a villa in Antwerp for a family with children the guiding principle for Cy Peys was to ensure the incidence of as much natural light as possible. She also strove for harmony by allowing various rooms to run into each other with new materials and by creating new entrances and proportions in the various rooms. All the materials were used honestly and purely: a rigorous and consistent whole. The intimacy of the dining room, as an exception to all other rooms, is put in the limelight a little more through the use of raffia on the walls. The uninterrupted sequence of all the functions is also very clearly present in this villa: living and dining room, kitchen, night corridor, bedrooms, etc. are all beautiful and well proportioned rooms that were connected harmoniously by Cy Peys.

www.cypeys.com

The playfulness is then again highlighted with a few distinctive elements (e.g. the chairs in the dining room).

White plastered walls make the spaces visually broader and more luminous.

↖
In this festival of white open spaces and light, the warm atmosphere is emphasised by the dark oak floors and the wengé furniture.

A SEASIDE APARTMENT

An apartment from the 1980's was converted by the interior architect Philip Simoen into a light and open holiday home. Lava rock from Dominique Desimpel was chosen as floor covering. All the custom made furniture was realised by D Interieur, the freestanding furniture (including an MDF table, Arper chairs, B&B sofas, Breuer chair, Bertoia barstools,…) is from Loft Living.

www.simoeninterieur.be

Furniture in painted MDF. Lighting by Modular.

The kitchen work surface was realised in Corian marble.

PERFECT INTEGRATION

This annex, designed by BoGarden in the idyllic surroundings of the Latemse Meersen, had to be able to accomodate several cars, but there had to be room, too, to be able to enjoy the wonderful location and the nearby house created by architect Xavier Donck. The building was erected on a traditional oak frame. All the outer walls are made of oak of varying widths.

www.xavierdonck.com   www.bogarden.be

BLENDING IN WITH THE LANDSCAPE

This house was built six years ago in a location with a magnificent panoramic views.
As the years passed, the owners realised that their love of cooking, entertaining guests and
enjoying the best that life has to offer was going to necessitate some changes to the building.
In the original house, the kitchen and dining room were strictly separated and Heritage
Buildings were given the rather complex task of creating a new combined space.
The consignment consisted of designing and building: a carport, a storage
space for wood, a kitchen extension including a dining area, a pool house
with a sauna and a covered terrace with a view of the swimming pool.

www.heritagebuildings.be

The hayloft door on the covered terrace provides access to a loft that is an ideal storage space.

The old joinery techniques used for the oak beams lends the building that typical «Heritage» atmosphere.

ANCIENT CHARM

When Karl Storms took over the company that his father Rik had founded more than thirty years ago, his first objective was to continue the excellent reputation of the family company. Just like his father (who had learned a lot from architect Raymond Rombouts), Karl has a passion for exceptional antique building materials and he integrates them into the exclusive projects of house owners and architects working in different styles: from classic and timeless to contemporary. Storms & Co supplies and places, coordinates and manages the workflow of these architectural antiques. The company has a large stock of authentic reclaimed materials, aged stones and wooden floors, antique fireplaces, roof tiles, natural stone, decorative and antique objects for the garden and the interior of the house.

www.rikstorms.com

ULTIMATE, MINIMALIST BEAUTY

The famous fashion designer Edouard Vermeulen (Natan) asked architects Marc
Corbiau and Vincent Van Duysen to design the interior of his Brussels apartment.

www.corbiau.com   www.vincentvanduysen.com

A CONTEMPORARY COUNTRY HOUSE

The Brussels interior design agency In Store was asked to transform a classic country house into a contemporary living environment.

www.instore.be

IN HARMONY

"Without emotion, there is no beauty" is the definition of elegance for the Themenos design studio. The Themenos designers believe that a classic interior suits all kinds of architecture: the essential starting point should always be a house with good proportions, regardless of its size or style.

www.themenos.be

Houses can always be elegant if proper consideration is given to the use of the space: they should not contain too many things, and the pieces that are chosen should harmonise with each other and with the home.

PURITY IN RURAL KEMPEN SURROUNDINGS

In this report, interior architect Alexis Herbosch introduces his own home, designed with the purity of country surroundings in mind. Contact between the rooms was most important, as was the view of the garden offered by the many windows around the house. This design studio appeals to all kinds of clients with its formula for creating atmosphere. Whether the project involves an English cottage, a long-fronted farmhouse in Kempen, a modern loft or an aristocratic eighteenth-centuryhouse, Herbosch - Van Reeth incorporates clients' ideas and wishes in all of its interior designs.

www.herbosch-vanreeth.be

Poplar planks ensure a serene atmosphere in the entrance
hall. The door to the cellar is concealed and has a section
that serves as a cat flap. A smoothed bluestone in a large
format was selected for the floor, laid in irregular bond.
The sliding door in the living room can screen off the open spaces
and creates a cosy atmosphere around the open fireplace.

The wall behind the gas stove is in black zeliges. These
display a clear contrast with the poplar wood, which
can be seen here again in the wooden kitchen units.
The cooking island is in the centre of the kitchen and
reinforces the feeling of connection with the garden.
The work surface is in smoothed bluestone.
The solid-oak table ('t Able) in the dining room
is also a creation by the design studio.

THE TIMELESS CACHET OF UNUSUAL WOODEN FLOORS

The family company Corvelyn is the point of reference for renowned architects, interior designers and private individuals who are looking for exclusive plank floors and parquets. This company from Aalter produces plank floors in new and old woods, such as oak, pitch-pine, elm, teak and more exotic varieties.
An expert on historic construction materials, Jan Corvelyn goes in search of unusual lots of wood, such as wide planks in old exotic wood from Sri Lanka, antique parquet from a Bulgarian barracks, wide pine boards from granaries in the Jura, beautiful broad brushed planks from a warehouse in Nancy and antique stairs from Fontainebleau.

www.corvelyn.be

For this orangery in a grand country house, Corvelyn used reclaimed teak planks from old houses in Indonesia. The wooden floor was glued and nailed onto an 18mm sheet of OSB with a joist structure beneath. The nails are almost invisible and serve only to hold the planks in place while the glue dries. Granular insulation has been inserted between the joists. The wooden floor fits perfectly with the wrought-iron windows and is level with the terrace, so that there is no doorstep when the windows are open.

↖
The clean lines create an
airy atmosphere, with no
rough and rustic feeling,
completely in harmony with
the English garden.

A PERFECT SYMBIOSIS

The success of this project is to a large extent a result of the excellent relationship between the clients and the team of Jan Verlinden, a dynamic family company that in recent years has concentrated on the construction and restoration of special gardens. Both parties realised that the swimming pool, the pool house and the terraces had to be integrated into the landscape in a completely natural way, as though they had always been there.

info@ballmore.com

The pool house was designed by the client and constructed using reclaimed materials throughout (oak planks and beams, reclaimed Boom tiles and Dutch clinkers).

THE CHARM OF OAK-FRAMED BUILDINGS

On the English countryside, oak-framed buildings such as stables, barns and other
outbuildings make for centuries an essential part of the changing landscape.
A few years ago, Peter Pollet and Koen Bouteligier decided to breathe new
life into the old craft of building with oak timbers on the continent.
Not only poolhouses, but also carports, guest houses, sheds, etc. are made by the team.

www.heritagebuildings.be

Traditional materials and craftsmanship are combined in original and timeless designs.
Only timberjointing methods are used, tightening the joints to give a uniquely strong structure.
Heritage Buildings operates in Belgium, the Netherlands, France and Germany. They can take care of a full build service, but their models can also be delivered as a kit.

A POOL HOUSE WITH ASIAN INFLUENCES

This pool house, designed by Nathalie Van Reeth, has been built in soaked afrormosia wood in order to create a more Asian emphasis. In its simplicity, this pool house fits in well with the surroundings and with the more classic family home. The space available for the construction of this pool house was limited. However, this outbuilding still offers sufficient space to have a shower or to enjoy the sauna and hammam in peace and quiet.

nathalie.vanreeth@skynet.be

The furniture inside is also made of afrormosia. The walls have been clad with rough whitewashed planks.

The large couch is covered with a waterproof material. Behind the wall is a sauna and a hammam with two open showers. The floor in flat stones runs throughout the whole building.

A STREAMLINED DESIGNER
APARTMENT IN THE UNITED STATES

Bruce Bananto is a renowned interior designer based in New York. For this project, he worked with EA2 (European Architectural Antiques), an international company specialising in traditional construction materials from Europe. The result is a minimalist mix of European and American style in a streamlined designer apartment.

ea2@me.com   www.bananto.com

The kitchen is a design by architect Bruce A. Wood of Boston (MA). The chairs are by Italian designer Gio Ponti. Table designed by Bruce Bananto, made of Corian and stainless steel.

The dining table was designed by architect Bruce Bananto and custom built by EA2. The dining chairs are by Mario Bellini.

SPACE AND LIGHT IN HARMONY

A young couple with three children built this luxurious house, together with Crepain Binst architectural studio. They called upon the services of 'aksent for the complete interior design. It was important that the clean, modern lines of the apartment should not become too chilly and cold. Stefan Paeleman from 'aksent took a contemporary approach that differs significantly from the normal designer look. The words 'past' and 'future' were important themes here. In line with the philosophy of their favourite design firm Promemoria, the link with the past ensures a sense of calm, whilst the future brings excitement and expectation.

www.aksent-gent.be

This semi-transparent sliding door in dark oak leads to the dressing room and bathroom and creates an intimate atmosphere.

↗
Colour and sophistication are the key themes in the living room.

↖
The chairs are in silk. Leather, bronze and precious woods also set the tone. The carpet is a combination of linen and silk. The curtains introduce a sense of casual informality. All of the furniture is by Romeo Sozzi.
Tall sliding doors with bronze handles separate the various spaces.

The library is one of the few closed parts of the house.

FIREPLACES MADE TO ORDER

The family firm De Puydt has been setting trends in contemporary interiors
with its open fireplaces for thirty years. These fireplaces combine the pleasure
of brilliant design with the assurance of modern technology.
De Puydt's fireplaces are professionally installed by company-trained
specialists, on the basis of a precise work plan and an agreed budget.

www.depuydthaarden.be

A gas fireplace was selected for this house with a minimalist design.

↖
A gas fire in a house designed by architect Marc Corbiau.

A WORTHY SUCCESSOR

In 1972, Andreas Van Apers founded a company dealing in historic construction materials that grew over thirty-five years to become one of Belgium's leading companies in this sector. On 1 May, 2008, his son Joris took over the business. The new company, Joris Van Apers bvba, continues his father's tradition, but also introduces completely new elements: the antique construction materials are incorporated into complete projects, with techniques for patination and ageing also playing an important role. The result: a most harmonious look in a timeless setting, with top-quality materials, traditional techniques and a large dose of creativity and technical know-how.

www.vanapers.be

All of the hinges and metal fittings are faithful 18th-century reproductions.

↖
These shelves, panelling and wooden floor create a warm, cosy atmosphere, combining original elements and new fitted woodwork.

EXCLUSIVE ARCHITECTURAL HARDWARE

"Hey, this is really special. Do you think you could get reproductions made?" asked architect Stéphane Boens when he discovered a collection of old architectural hardware in Peter van Cronenburg's car one day about twelve years ago. Peter van Cronenburg, at the time a specialist in shelving, panelling and interior doors, had bought the pieces during a tour of England. He had long felt frustrated because he was unable to find suitable fittings to lend the finishing touches to his work. He felt that what was available was either too modern or too nineteenth-century, or there was something artificial about the finish. So he decided that if it wasn't available, he'd go out and find it for himself.

www.petervancronenburg.be

Architectural hardware forms an essential element of any room, combining with form, colour, proportion, light and texture to create a harmonious atmosphere.

SYMBIOSIS ARCHITECT – CRAFTSMAN

Peter van Cronenburg assesses every design for its significance, attractiveness, function and proportions. The collection now includes over 7000 pieces, from 16th-century Venetian door handles to American Shaker pieces, from Louis XIV knobs to Art Deco doorbells and taps. Simple design and high quality are always top priorities.

www.petervancronenburg.be

The elegant "Julia" handle seems to be an echo of the work of art on the left.

Within the same room, there can be a variation in the shapes of the handles, to suit the function of each cupboard.

↖
The doors have a fine, streamlined lock.

PERFECTION EVEN
IN THE SMALLEST DETAILS

Over the past twenty years, Dauby nv has gained a strong reputation as Europe's leading importer of exclusive door fittings. The company offers a wide range of high-quality articles, specialising in original, traditionally manufactured designs of days gone by and shunning the many copies that have flooded the market. Dauby guarantees quality fittings that lend charm and elegance to any interior, no matter what the architectural style.

www.dauby.be

Authentic fittings are imported from countries including Italy, France and Spain. In rustic, country-style collections, authenticity is extremely important. Both the materials and the way in which the fittings are made play an important part. The fittings may be made from metals including solid bronze, traditional wrought iron or the exclusive Britannium metal. The fittings are cast in sand moulds and finished by hand. These small details make a world of difference in every chic and sophisticated interior.
Created by Paul Rijs.

A CONTEMPORARY FACELIFT
FOR A CLASSIC HOME

Interior architect Stephanie Laporte (The Office Belgium) was commissioned
to give a facelift to this elegant home in Ieper (Ypres).
This grand house underwent a complete metamorphosis, with its classic
architecture giving way to a minimalist and streamlined contemporary look.

www.stephanielaporte.be

The cloakroom, with its cupboards in matte lacquered MDF and sliding doors with built-in handles. In the background, the guest toilet with a mosaic floor and velvet curtain. The oak floor has a bleached finish.

↗
The sofas were specially designed for this project, with a coffee table in dark wood. A pale oak floor and velvet curtains.

↖
A view from the sitting room into the dining room.

Stephanie Laporte also designed everything in the bar. Wall units in dark wood, combined with a mirror and lacquered glass. A light with a cascade of crystal chains.

MONOCHROME WHITE

This report shows a project by the interior designer Dominique Koch
(Zoute Nostalgie) in an almost monochrome white colour pallet.

THE INTERACTION EXTERIOR / INTERIOR

The interaction between the exterior and interior of a house is of the utmost importance to the young group of architects and interior designer Themenos.

www.themenos.be

ARTISTIC INSPIRATION

This 18th-century farmhouse has been carefully restored by the artist Daan van Doorn, a famous painter of portraits.

www.jobinterieur.nl   www.daanvandoorn.com

REINTERPRETATION OF A FRENCH MANOIR

In this project, Themenos reinterprets the timeless beauty of the classic French manoir.

www.themenos.be

A MODERN INTERPRETATION OF
AN 18TH-CENTURY FARMHOUSE

Architect Stéphane Boens created this farmhouse in the same style as those built in East Flanders in the eighteenth century. However, the interior of this farmhouse has a surprisingly contemporary design: the ceilings, some as high as three metres, create a great sense of space, which, together with the streamlined design, ensures a modern and timeless atmosphere. This is the ideal living environment for a family with three young children.

www.stephaneboens.be

The entrance hall sets the tone: rough wooden floors, a subdued colour scheme and traditional craftsmanship.

INTERIOR CONCEPTS FULL OF CHARACTER

In business for thirty years, Antiques & Design has grown to become the port of call for the renovation and adaptation of custom-made antique pine furniture. This Kempen company's profile was raised after it provided interiors for the branches of the well-known bakery and café chain Le Pain Quotidien, including worldwide shops in the United States. In recent years, Antiques & Design has increasingly focused on creating private interiors: from design to construction.

www.antiques-design.be

Based on a project by architect Stéphane Boens. Solid oak panels made from reclaimed wood. The English skirting boards are also made from solid oak. Rusted old door furniture based on an English design.

↗ This solid oak panelling has been patinated.

↖ Antiques & Design installed old oak panelling and shutters in this salon.

Old pine bookshelves, originally from France.

DISTINCTIVE TOTAL INTERIORS
TAILORED TO THE CLIENT

Every Antiques & Design interior is unique, whether it involves a kitchen, bathroom, dressing room, library or any other space. The combination of the client's wishes with the ideas of the design team and the use of one-off old elements lends each creation a personal, distinctive feel.

www.antiques-design.be

A stair in old oak with a small wrought iron window.

↖

This old staircase from a Limburg
farmhouse has been carefully restored.
The shelving is made from an old French
shop-display unit.
All of the solid pine doors are from
Germany.

THE WARMTH OF RECLAIMED AND AGED WOOD

The company Deknock showcases several examples of the use
of reclaimed and aged timber in this report.
The photos perfectly illustrate the high standards
of quality that the company always achieves.

www.antiekdeknock.be

The beams are original:
panelling and floors
are in reclaimed oak.

A COUNTRY HOUSE IN PERFECT HARMONY
WITH NATURE

Since 1970, Vlassak-Verhulst have carried out over eight hundred exceptional residential projects of the highest quality. In recent years, the company has expanded to become the market leader in the construction of exclusive homes: an ideal partner for building projects, for whom quality, professionalism and customer satisfaction are of prime importance. Vlassak-Verhulst make the case for a timeless, classic style of construction with modest charm, perfectly in keeping with the landscape of the Low Countries. The country house in this report is a fine example of Vlassak-Verhulst's expertise: an atmospheric country home surrounded by nature in the green outskirts of Antwerp.

www.vlassakverhulst.com

The roof is clad with old blue Boom tiles and reed thatch.
Old, reclaimed paepesteen bricks laid in cross bond were chosen for the façade.

↖
At the back of the building,
a variety of windows draws
the attention. To the left is
the wooden corner window
of the kitchen, with a large
metal-framed cross window
next to it. A sliding wooden
door can be used to close
off the window of the living
room.

A pleasant working environment, with a lot of light and contact with the beautiful greenery of the garden.
The custom-made, painted wall-unit provides plenty of storage space.

Paepesteen bricks around the open fireplace.
The window in this living room provides contact to the surrounding nature all year round.

The window above the oak counter with its old sink allows a lot of light into the room.
The wall behind the oven has been clad with zeliges.
Simplicity, warmth, functionality and atmosphere in this kitchen, emphasised by the all-oak central unit that provides extra workspace.

Bathroom, dressing room and bedroom flow into one another. Painted cupboards and an oak floor in the dressing room and bedroom. The old oak truss reaches up into the ridge of the house.

THE RENOVATION
OF A POLDER FARMHOUSE

The aim of this renovation project was to make it appear as though this authentic farmhouse
had just been done up. But the farmhouse actually required complete renovation, which
was carried out with respect for the materials and the local style of construction.
The owners and their interior architect succeeded marvellously in achieving their goal.

The parents' bedroom with its dressing room and bathroom with a view of the garden.

The adjoining bathroom with washbasin blocks and a walk-in shower.

RUSTIC INSPIRATION

This countryside villa was designed by the Demyttenaere architectural studio from Knokke. Sand's Company, the interior-design firm that works closely with Demyttenaere, took care of the complete interior of this idyllically situated house.

www.myth.be   www.sandscompany.be

The wall behind the fireplace is in brushed, white-oiled French oak. The fireplace has a surround of Pietra Piasentina natural stone.

The cupboard unit and the wall behind the bed are in sandblasted and stained oak veneer.

SOBER REFINEMENT
IN A CLASSIC FRENCH MANOIR

This classic French manoir in the leafy outskirts of Antwerp was constructed by Costermans.
The company devoted the utmost attention to the selection of materials, installing unusual
antique tiles, durable old parquet floors, exceptional fireplaces and other special details.
The look is timeless, yet contemporary: a sober and sophisticated living environment.

www.costermans-projecten.be

The sitting room with an old French oak parquet floor in Hungarian point.

The salon with its historic French Louis XV fireplace.
Natural materials have been combined with a bright green accent.

BLENDING WITH THE LANDSCAPE

All of the elements of this project have blended into the surrounding natural landscape:
the old farmhouse that gives the impression of having been there for centuries,
the two extensions (the garage and the kitchen), which were built by Heritage
Buildings, and the garden, which merges perfectly with the rural surroundings.

www.heritagebuildings.be

Heritage Buildings transformed the kitchen space, originally a small area, into a fully fledged kitchen-cum-dining room. The oak structure is held together with mortise and tenon joints; there are no nails involved at all. The truss, open right up into the ridge of the roof, creates an authentic, rustic atmosphere.

The large windows provide a 180° view of the garden. All of the pipes and cables have been concealed within the wooden interior planking.

↖
The oak extension by Heritage Buildings blends seamlessly with the garden. As soon as the temperature outside allows, the doors are opened wide.
Over time, the wooden planking outside has gained a beautiful silver-grey patina.

ENGLISH INSPIRATION

This country house is the second created by architect Stéphane Boens in English style.

www.stephaneboens.be

RESTORATION OF A NINETEENTH-CENTURY
FARMHOUSE WITH A COURTYARD

Architect Bernard De Clerck has restored and adapted a dilapidated early nineteenth-century
farmhouse to accommodate the needs of a young family with a number of children.
The clients acquired this spacious property because of their great love for
nature and for pets: they keep horses, ponies, dogs and chickens.
This has resulted in a coherent whole that is carefully integrated into the rural surroundings.
The entire house has been renovated; reclaimed materials
were used and the roof has been replaced.

info@bernarddeclerck.be

The main room has been fitted with eighteenth-century pitch-pine panelling and beautifully carved decorative frames.

DISCREET RESTORATION
OF AN EIGHTEENTH-CENTURY "GENTILHOMMIÈRE"

For over a decade, Edouard Vermeulen (Natan), the renowned couturier,
has lived on the Rozenhout estate: an eighteenth-century country
house, or "gentilhommière", situated in glorious parkland.
In close collaboration with the architect Raymond Rombouts, the
original house was improved and a pavilion added.
Edouard Vermeulen – himself an interior designer before he made his name
in the world of haute couture – took care of the interior decoration:
a timeless and subtle colour palette, in the same spirit as his exclusive collections.

The seating and the cupboard were selected by antique dealers Brigitte and Alain Garnier.

↑
The fully panelled bathroom, designed according to an original idea from Raymond Rombouts.

↖
The panelling also comes from Stéphane de Harlez. They have been adapted for this room by the architect Rombouts.

An almost monastic sense of calm and simplicity.

MODESTY AND SPACE:
A RESTORED COUNTRY HOUSE IN FLANDERS

When renovating this initially unpromising farmhouse and barn in Flanders, architect Vincent Van Duysen strived to maintain the serene and homely rural character of the house. So, the emphasis in the interior was subtly placed on the country surroundings. Purely to emphasise the spatial qualities, he introduced some large windows looking onto the modest, green garden. With the simple interplay of views, circulation axes and different ceiling heights, the architect creates a fascinating space that does not fall within everyday expectations. The sober, yet warm choice of colours and materials reinforces this effect.

www.vincentvanduysen.com

A Vincent Van Duysen lamp, made from old glass and black ironwork, hangs from the double-height ceiling in the living room.

The bathroom of the parents' bedroom, in fired bluestone, was completely designed by Vincent Van Duysen. The artwork is a photo by Robert Mapplethorpe.

↖
An untreated natural oak floor has been laid in the living room. The panelling is made of solid natural pine boards that have been stained.

The panelling in the parents' bedroom is made of solid natural pine boards that have been stained.

SIMPLE SOPHISTICATION IN HIGH-TECH SURROUNDINGS

Stephanie Laporte of The Office Belgium was asked to take care of the interior design of this house created by Marc Corbiau for a young family with three children. She worked in close collaboration with Obumex. The owners wanted a practical, extremely comfortable home: bright, simple and cosy, with lots of natural light and made of basic, but very reliable materials. The same materials were used throughout: dark natural stone for the floor and the washstand in the cloakroom; tinted and brushed oak veneer for the cupboards and solid-oak parquet flooring. The lighting also plays an important role, and a great deal of attention was paid to the latest technology in audio and video, lighting control, security, video phones and air conditioning with touch-screen operation, internet and specially made key panels (designed and created by Dubois Ctrl – air conditioning and automation concepts).

www.stephanielaporte.be   www.obumex.be   www.duboiscontrol.be

The custom-built oak stairs have been tinted in the same shade as the wooden floor.

All of the office wall-units and the oak-veneer desk were made to order by Devaere. Promemoria lamp (from Obumex) and fully integrated air conditioning (via the subtle openings in the ceiling).

A view from the upstairs corridor (with art by Fred Boffin) into the bedroom, which has been finished in oak veneer.

The dressing room is also in oak veneer.

Curtains by Bruder, bedside lights by Dubois Ctrl.

SOBER WHITE AND DARK SHADES
IN A MODERN DUPLEX APARTMENT

Stephanie Laporte from The Office Belgium designed the interior of this contemporary duplex apartment in West Flanders. The clients, a young couple, wanted a simple, contemporary interior with warm tones. As the apartment is completely enclosed and not much light comes in from outside, the home was finished in pale shades throughout, with a few darker accents for features including the wooden floor and the hall cupboard. The decision to use one model of light fitting throughout the whole apartment also creates a peaceful, calming atmosphere. Obumex and Kordekor were commissioned to carry out the project.

www.stephanielaporte.be   www.obumex.be   www.groepkordekor.com

The white walls contrast with the dark-tinted oak floor.

The custom-built oak stairs have been tinted in the same shade as the wooden floor.

↖
The central features of the living room are the sofas covered with material from Sahco Hesslein around a coffee table from JNL. Zinc. Limited Edition carpet. Seating with integrated heating and a wall unit with a desk and a TV recess, made of bleached oak veneer (Obumex).

Dining table and chairs in dark-tinted maple with leather (JNL). The light fitting was produced specially by Modular. Fitted wall units with integrated central heating (by Obumex). Baumann roller blinds to provide shade have been combined with panels by Sahco Hesslein.

The bedroom, with its dominant dark shades and a few white accents, contrasts with the rest of this duplex apartment: Sahco Hesslein curtains and a JNL chair with Designers Guild fabric. All of the furniture has been matt-painted in the same dark shades as the walls.

A SUBTLE PALETTE OF COLOURS
IN A SPACIOUS PENTHOUSE

Philip Simoen was commissioned to furnish this penthouse, which has a floor area of over 350m². The resulting look shows the preference of this interior architect from West Flanders for simple design with a warm atmosphere: subtle nuances of colour harmonising with fine materials (such as natural stone, silk velvet, bronze and tinted oak) in sophisticated contemporary surroundings.

www.simoeninterieur.be

An aged-oak parquet floor has been laid throughout the hall (Vanrobaeys). The console was made to order. Lola lighting.

↗ The tinted-oak desk was made to order and designed by Philip Simoen. The bronze table lamp and the standard lamps are by Christian Liaigre.

↖ Promemoria chairs, covered in silk velvet. Fitted shelving units in bleached, sandblasted oak. Curtains by Romo (Linara), made by Inndekor. A gas fire by De Puydt.

The dressing is a Philip Simoen creation.

A SENSE OF SPACE

This magical place, situated in the heart of Brussels, has a view that certainly stands comparison with any metropolis. It used to be an office space on the roof of a residential building, but it has now been converted into a wonderful apartment with a garden and terraces and a floor area of 500 m². The apartment was designed by Nathalie Delabye for Ensemble & Associés and furnished throughout by Isabelle Reynders with creations by Christian Liaigre. In consultation with the client, who is just as enthusiastic as the designers about the "invisible" details, this space has been transformed into a place where purity and simplicity harmonise with a real sense of well-being.

www.ensembleetassocies.be   www.christian-liaigre.fr

White leather "Autan" couch by Christian Liaigre. Wrought-iron open fireplace. A "Murdoch" méridienne in linen and white leather by Christian Liaigre.

The living room is also used for film screenings. A gas fire and furniture by Christian Liaigre: an "Augustin" chair in linen and silk, "Buddha" armchairs and low "Galet" tables in white leather. The shelving unit (p. 204-205) was specially made in sandblasted oak that has been stained white.

↖
A view from the entrance hall, panelled throughout in white-stained sandblasted oak, of the stairs leading to the dining room, terrace and garden.

"Celtic" table in stained oak by Christian Liaigre.
"Archipel" chairs in stained oak and white leather, also by Christian Liaigre.
In the background is the "floating" garden.

The desk was also made to order in white-stained sandblasted oak. White leather Eames desk chair.

The master bedroom and en-suite dressing room, fitted throughout with white-stained sandblasted oak, provides access to the bathroom and the living room/film room.

HAUTE COUTURE IN A HOME IN THE HEART OF PARIS

A few months after the opening of Ebony Interiors' new Paris showroom,
Gilles de Meulemeester completed the company's first project in Paris. The result is
shown in this report: a sitting room, dining room, TV room, bathroom and bedroom
in a home in the heart of Paris where all of the pieces are custom made:
Ebony has made such "haute couture" work a company hallmark.

www.ebony-interiors.com

A Broadway dining table and Bruxelles chairs. The radiator grilles, carpet and hanging lamp are custom-made pieces by Ebony.

A carpet in wool, linen and cotton in the TV room.

THE CONTEMPORARY RENOVATION
OF AN AUTHENTIC FAMILY HOME

This country house, which was furnished around
ten years ago by the late Jean de Meulder,
has recently been redesigned by Gilles de Meulemeester.
He also added a new wing in the original spirit of the house.

www.ebony-interiors.com

The bathroom was specially built in natural stone and oak.

A dressing table with drawers and a leather-covered seat in the bathroom.

↖
The office of the lady of the house: cabinetwork and desk designed by Gilles de Meulemeester. In the centre is a Bulhul statue from the Philippines.

A COUNTRY HOUSE DESIGNED IN A HISTORIC STYLE

Architect Bernard De Clerck dreamed up a story when he created this newly built project: a story about the changes that a 17th-century country home might have undergone. A large one-storey house has been converted to add an upper storey. A barn has been turned into a coach house. And then, in around 1780, this coach house and the main house were linked together with a 'plaisance' pavilion to cater to the needs of a family with growing children. And this is how this harmonious collection of buildings came about, situated around an inner courtyard.

This story, which sprang from the architect's imagination, formed the basis of the project, which is perfectly integrated into its park surroundings. Construction firm: Hyboma / Artebo.

info@bernarddeclerck.be

The formal dining room
is panelled with painted
wood.

↑
The garden room in the 'plaisance'
pavilion. One wall has been
clad in aged pitch-pine planks
with concealed cupboards
and steps up to the library.

The library/workroom
up in the roof of the
'plaisance' pavilion.

A BLEND OF TIMELESS AND CONTEMPORARY:
A BALANCED PHILOSOPHY FOR LIVING

This farmhouse was created by architect Stéphane Boens.
The owners also use the house as a showroom for am projects, their interior-design company.
Their work is more a philosophy of life than simply decoration.
They create timeless environments and living spaces that are perfectly in balance
with the lifestyle of their clients. They decorated this house themselves.

www.amprojects.be   www.stephaneboens.be

Am projects has a unique collection of products for use in the garden and around the swimming pool.

A sauna, shower, lavatory and changing room have been integrated into the pool house.

↖
The owners/designers opted to create a close connection between their house and the landscape.

A work by Renaat Ivens above an 18th-century Provençal commode.

The entrance hall has a monastic feel to it. Am projects often incorporate modern art into their designs. This is a work by Michel Mouffe.

A number of 18th-century os de mouton walnut chairs were restored and reupholstered by am projects. These have been combined with a table by Norman Foster and an Eames desk chair.

The master
bedroom and
adjoining dressing
room have an
almost meditative
ambience. The
boxspring bed and
the sofa bed were
made specially and
upholstered by am
projects.

The bedroom
corridor has
a monastic
charm. Above:
this Bradford
American pool
table with Queen
Anne legs is also
distributed by am
projects.

On the wall are artworks by Jörg Döring.

THE METAMORPHOSIS OF VILLA MARIE

Obumex was responsible for the complete redesign of Villa Marie. Kurt Neirynck (senior interior architect at Obumex) brought about a real metamorphosis over the two years of renovation work. This classic cottage has been redone throughout and considerably extended under the direction of architect Xavier Donck. The space has also been divided up in a more contemporary style. The library was created by Axel Vervoordt. Paintwork by Dankers Decor. Kurt Neirynck designed the interior and coordinated the work in close collaboration with the client. Personal notes create a sense of well-being in this distinctive house.

www.obumex.be

The client uses the library as a workspace. A kilim from Azerbaijan (Iran) and a collection of old legal texts accentuate the atmosphere. The antique desk came from the Banque de France.

THE COMPLETE TRANSFORMATION
OF A BELLE EPOQUE COUNTRY HOUSE

This Belle Epoque country house was built in three phases. The original house was a modestly proportioned hunting lodge dating from 1890. Two more sections were added in 1904 and 1920. The house has recently undergone a painstaking process of restoration, under the enthusiastic direction of the owner. She has renovated the historic country house in a 'gentle' way, full of respect for the authentic architectural elements of the property. The surrounding park garden (over two hectares) has also been completely transformed and restored to its former glory, in close collaboration with Ballmore landscape architects (tree nursery/creation and restoration of timeless gardens).

info@ballmore.com

All of the panelling and the plaster fireplaces are new, but were made in keeping with the architectural style of the house.

The old oak floor has been restored.

↖
Large and high rooms, furnished in an almost monastic style. The modular sofa and pouf are by Flexform (model: Ground Piece).

SPACE AND SUBTLE LUXURY
IN A SCULPTURAL VILLA

Custom-built interiors are Obumex's area of unmatchable expertise. This house, designed by the
Brussels architect Fabien Van Tomme, is an example of the company's approach. The garden
and surroundings are by Buro Groen. Xavier Gadeyne, senior interior architect at Obumex,
designed and supervised all of the interior work. Sumptuous materials, subtle colours and
impressive spaces make this home and office a place of luxury and relaxation. Complemented by
modern art from the owner's collection, this house forms a timeless and contemporary whole.

www.obumex.be

Serene, white walls and a bleached, aged oak parquet floor throughout. Art by Albert Mastenbroek (this page) and Jörg Döring (right page).

↑
This pivoting mirrored door at the end of the upstairs corridor creates an impression of space.

↖
Sitting area with black Promemoria sofas and white leather armchairs by Christian Liaigre on a cotton carpet. Gas fire with a low view through to the swimming pool.

The parents' bathroom with two 'Wash' washstands, designed by Vincent Van Duysen for Obumex.

Reading corner with chaises longues by Christian Liaigre. Fitted floor-to-ceiling cupboards.

UNDERSTATED ELEGANCE
IN THE GREEN OUTSKIRTS OF ANTWERP

A rather dull French-style house from the 1960s was transformed to create a spacious, up-to-date home that fulfils all of the client's requirements for comfort. Light and (breathing) space were key elements of this design. So as to allow the house to develop more character, hardwood that will evolve naturally with the surroundings was selected for the windows. Materials that develop a patina over time are also a feature of the interior. This means that the house will lead a life of its own and the aesthetic qualities of the space will increase. The roof was also thoroughly remodelled in order to create more space. This whole upper storey can now be used optimally. The alterations even made it possible to install a mezzanine floor in the rooms of the two teenagers. The sense of calm and understatement in this home is remarkable. 'Aksent have turned their philosophy into reality in this strong combination of functionality and emotion.

www.aksent-gent.be

This room serves as a TV room and bar. The bright-red lacquered cupboard is a reference to fashionable bar decor. The furniture is by Flexform.

The custom-built hardwood shelving with a silk back is in direct contact with the garden. Furniture by Promemoria: the armchair and the stitching on the leather desk is in sky blue.

↖
This low window seamlessly connects interior and exterior. The pond in the courtyard reinforces the sense of calm in this understated living room. When the sun is shining, the light on the water creates enchanting reflections on the ceiling inside. The armchair and bronze occasional tables are by Promemoria.

A GREAT SENSE OF HARMONY

Without a doubt, Elbchaussee in Hamburg is one of the most beautiful avenues in Germany. Extending around ten kilometres along the banks of the Elbe, it is adorned with nineteenth-century and modern villas, all surrounded by enormous private parks. People drive down the avenue at thirty kilometres per hour so as to be able to admire all of the beautiful buildings that have been constructed here and to enjoy the magnificent view over the Elbe at the same time. Walking through the rooms of this impressive villa, visitors can enjoy the colour palette and the wonderful decoration throughout this entire interior. Everything has been finished perfectly, right down to the smallest detail. The architecture and the garden have been painstakingly attuned with the spectacular location of the site, with a great sense of harmony. This magnificent villa is unique in every respect.

www.vlassakverhulst.com

A wooden floor in old
Bordeaux oak.
Curtains in heavy beige
linen and yellow velvet.

The oak desk has been
painted, floor in old
Avignon oak, laid in
Hungarian point.
Upholstery and furniture
in harmony with the
atmosphere and colours
of the room.

The dining room, with
ceiling-height contoured
panelling.
On the floor, a Versailles
parquet in old oak.

Floor in old Bordeaux
planks. The oak dresser
has a painted finish.
Linen curtains by Ralph
Lauren.

↖
The ceiling-height panelling
in the winter sitting room is in
brushed French oak.
The painting above the fireplace
conceals a flatscreen TV.

The first floor.
Walls with
contoured
panelling.
The curved
French-oak
staircase leading
to the attic has a
patinated finish.
Fabric blinds by
Beacon Hill.

The lady's dressing rooms in Bordeaux old oak.

↑
The pine cupboards in
the master bathroom
have a patinated finish.

The mirror by the bath
conceals a TV.

A SOPHISTICATED PUZZLE

This house, built in the 1960s in the Antwerpse Kempen region of Belgium, was given a new look by AIDarchitecten, refurbished and extended to include a new children's section on top of the existing house. The construction of the interior is based on a rhythm of three with doors and cupboards fitting into a brick grid and blending into the architecture of the house. The architecture has a basic kit form; the interior is a sophisticated puzzle that fits inside it. The right proportions and the grid of the columns ensure that the house has a natural look and a calming atmosphere.

www.aidarchitecten.be

The stairs, with their compactness and simplicity, are in themselves an image of individuality.

The compact kitchen forms the heart of this home.

↖
The furnishings are reduced to their essence: natural and light materials have been selected. The distinctive furniture contrasts with the informal design of the custom-made pieces.

A STATELY COUNTRY HOUSE

This stately country house was built in 1914 and has a living area of
850m² on a site with a parkland garden of three hectares.
During the renovation work, which was managed by Q&M, the style
of the house was taken into consideration, but the whole building was
brought up to date with cleaner lines and a fusion of styles.

walter.quirynen@skynet.be

The TV room is beside the library. A sliding door can be used to separate the two spaces. The TV room has the latest Dolby Surround systems.
All carpets by Bomat.

↖
The library, with its beautiful wooden panelling, has a warm atmosphere. A B&I creation.

↑
The dining area by the kitchen. The combination of streamlined lighting and classic chairs is particularly distinctive.

The kitchen (an Apart Keukens creation) is also a combination of modern and older elements. The Carrara marble lends the room a fresh atmosphere.
The chandelier is the eye-catching feature here. The large refrigerator by Amana adds a striking accent.

A HOUSE NEAR THE DUTCH COAST

Vlassak-Verhulst, the exclusive villa construction company, built
this stately country house with a number of outbuildings.
The house, situated in magnificent natural surroundings near Bergen aan
Zee (Dutch coast), was then handed over to Sphere Concepts, who assumed
responsibility for the entire design and creation of the interior.

www.vlassakverhulst.com   www.sphereconcepts.be

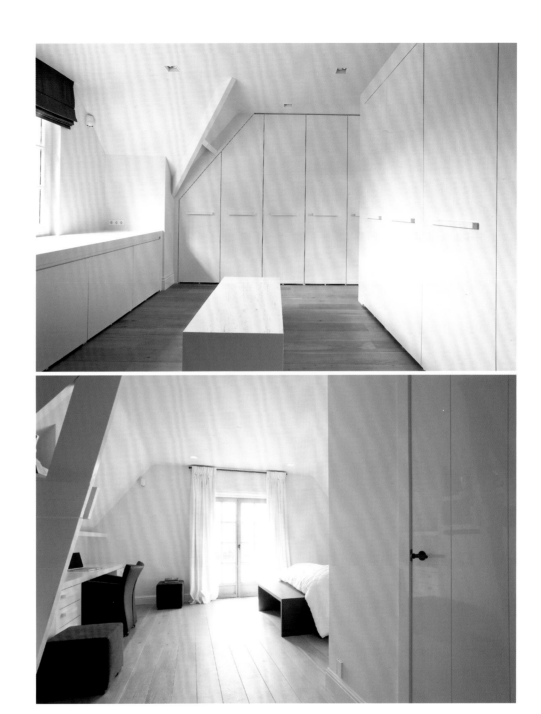

A RESPECTFUL RESTORATION

This old farmhouse, situated in the green outskirts of Antwerp on a castle estate, has recently been completely restored by AIDarchitecten (G. Van Zundert / K. Bakermans). The house is in idyllic countryside, with a garden of several hectares that merges with the surrounding nature. The restoration was kept as authentic as possible, with no superfluous adornment: the aim was to create a calm living environment for a young, dynamic family, with a focus on functionality and space. This no-nonsense approach has resulted in a simple and honest atmosphere. The use of old, natural materials in combination with some contemporary elements has also helped to create a special, distinctive feel in this home.

www.aidarchitecten.be

↖
The various outbuildings
have modern functions,
including storage space,
a covered terrace, a pool
house, and a garage/studio.

Contemporary works of art by Denmark and Jan Dries contrast with the mix of rustic oak furniture, individual pieces by Scandinavian modernists and highlights of modern design.

The owners' imagination and the successful collaboration have created an interior that is a unique blend of streamlined furnishings and fittings, combined with exclusive reclaimed construction materials.

The interior merges beautifully with the architecture, in light and natural materials.

Magnificent views of the garden combine with harmonious decor throughout the property.

167

A HAVEN OF TRANQUILLITY

A haven of tranquillity set at the heart of a 6-hectare park on the outskirts of Brussels: the countryside at the town's doorstep. Transformed by the architects A.R.P.E (Antoine de Radiguès) and the general construction firm Macors, this small, resolutely New England-style manor house is dedicated to harmony. With noble materials, large rooms, daring decorative creations from Lionel Jadot and green spaces completely redesigned by Michel Delvosalle … the constant interaction between the house and the surrounding natural environment is clear for all to see. Only experienced professionals well versed in their respective trades have been used to carry out the work to the interior decor, to redesign the land and to transform the house itself. This is evident even in the smallest of details.

lioneljadot@yahoo.fr   www.macors.be

Great attention has been paid to every detail to ensure the comfort of the manor residents; for example, the bedrooms have access to an outdoor Jacuzzi on the first floor where the residents can relax.
There are also comfortable lounge chairs (Royal Botania) on the ground floor for relaxation and an Indonesian bench provides an area for daydreaming…

↖
The roof of the terrace is supported by oak pillars which have been coated. At nightfall, the terrace is lit up by beautiful lanterns created by Vincent Van Duysen.

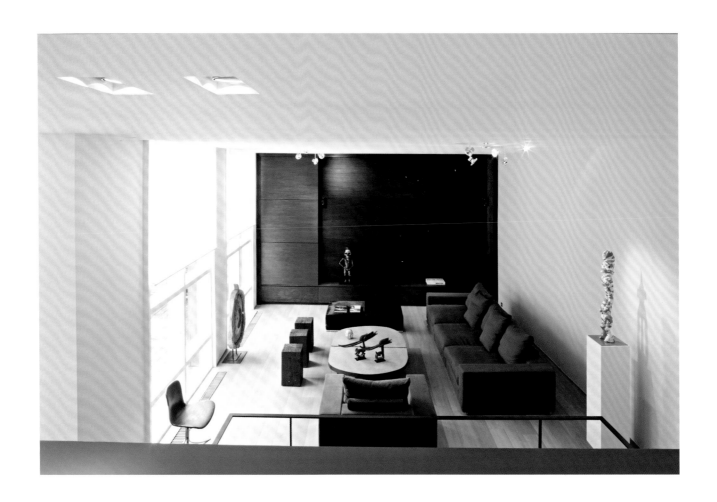

OPENING UP THE SPACE

This loft on two storeys is situated in the heart of Brussels in a former studio with a house behind. The space was completely redesigned by the Olivier Dwek architectural studio in collaboration with architect Mathieu DeWitte. The creation of one single volume over the two floors ensures optimal light throughout the apartment and completely opens up the space. The library, with its monumental proportions and varying heights works as a living and functional object. It consists of two floors with built-in staircases. The owner's office is on the top floor. The kitchen retreats into the background, allowing the furnishings and the many works of art to stand out.

www.olivierdwek.com

Right, a Scandia chair by the Norwegian designer Hans Brattrud.
Black-and-white silver-gelatine prints by Thierry Le Gouès.

Chairs by the Danish designer Poul Kjaerholm (PK 9), manufactured
by Kold Christensen and found at the shop of antiques dealer Jerome
Sohier.
The brushed stainless-steel kitchen takes its inspiration from
industrial settings.
In the background, a work by German artist Jonathan Meese.
The table (with a surface in mosaic tiles in Pompeii lava) was
designed by Olivier Dwek.

A WARM AND CASUAL ATMOSPHERE

This report features the first phase of Daskal-Laperre Interior Architects' transformation of a classic house into a contemporary space that radiates a warm and casual atmosphere. The second phase of the renovation is still to come. The rooms of the house have been opened up to create more generous views throughout the building. Sliding doors can be used to separate the spaces. The interior designers Daskal and Laperre selected natural materials to create a sober look, almost monochrome with a palette of natural colours. The owners of this house are passionate about literature, so a large library occupies a central position. The plan is divided into three sections: a sitting room around the open fireplace with library shelving and workspace; a room between the kitchen and the sitting room with a TV corner and daybed in an alcove in front of the large window with its garden view; and, finally, a kitchen.

www.daskal-laperre.com

Sofas and armchairs designed by Axel Vervoordt.
The radiators are concealed behind grilles.

↑
A parquet floor in natural bleached oak. The sliding doors and the oak panels have been sanded and bleached. The daybed in the alcove looks out over the garden. The TV is concealed behind the wooden doors.

↖
The wooden blinds make it possible to filter the light.

All of the kitchen equipment can be hidden behind sliding doors. A solid wooden table, designed by the architects. Wegner chairs, hanging lamps in bronze by craftsman Jos Devriendt.

White linen curtains, coffee tables in ebony, designed by the architects.

STYLEFUL, HOSPITABLE, WARM

This classic residence clearly demands a stylish interior. Christel De Vos, proprietor of RR, here opted for collections from Flexform, Maxalto, Van Rossum, Zanotta,... The black and white combination of wrought-iron doors and the furniture has resulted in a peaceful and perfect whole. A stylish, hospitable and warm interior, which answers entirely to the wishes of the residents.

www.rrinterieur.be

A FAÇADE WITH A SEAVIEW

RR Interior Concepts, in cooperation with interior architect Nathalie
Deboel, provided a splendid apartment facing the sea.
A deliberate choice was made of furniture by Flexform, Minotti,
Van Rossum, in warm shades of orange and red.
The combination of light, colourful tints and wood gives a pleasant atmosphere,
offering a sense of warmth and security in summer and winter.

www.rrinterieur.be   www.nathaliedeboel.be

TIMELESS AND FORWARD-LOOKING

RR Interior Concepts stands for contemporary and timeless
interior design from famous brands and designers.

www.rrinterieur.be

FIAT LUX

Located at the back of a courtyard, this formerly rundown house suffered from lack of light. Consulted before the purchase, the Lempereurs were able to reassure the future owners that it could be turned into a luminous place. The challenge was significant: the house is only open on one side. The ingeniousness of the reconstruction can be seen in the multiplicity of new openings: windows, patio, inner windows, wider passageways and prospects. Today, the house is radiant. Its darker areas have been used in another way, turned into a cabinet with niches to display the head of household's collection of bronzes. The furniture, adjusted to each room, the lighting, and the refined wall-coverings all complete this spectacular renovation.

www.olivierlempereur.com

BEST OF BOTH WORLDS

A big-city, cosmopolitan atmosphere in green surroundings on the edge
of Brussels, yet still close to the city centre: this private residence, created
by architect Marc Corbiau, offers the best of both worlds.
Raoul Cavadias, a Belgian designer with Greek roots who was born in Africa
and grew up in Switzerland, took care of the interior design of this distinctive
city villa which radiates a sense of space, serenity and sophistication.

raoulcavadias@live.be   www.corbiau.com

The office and TV room.
Bleached teakwood panelling. The coffee
table and desk are by Liaigre.
The woven-leather lounge suite was designed
by Raoul Cavadias.

↖
The floor in the entrance hall is made
from Afghan sandstone.
A bench by Andrée Putman with
a windbreak in metal and rusty
chainmail in the background (created
by Raoul Cavadias).
The stair rail in brushed stainless steel
is also a design by Cavadias.

The master bedroom.
The walls of the corridor and
the dressing room and the
bedroom panelling were also
made in bleached teakwood
to a design by R. Cavadias.

A STRIKING CONTRAST

This house for a family with children is situated in a residential district.
There is a striking contrast between the building's rather
classic exterior and the contemporary interior.
The central entrance hall with its brick vaulted ceiling is the only
room in which the classic inspiration can still be seen.

www.stephanielaporte.be

Stretched fabric has
been used for the walls.
Custom-made lighting.
Table and chairs by
Promemoria. The slats
of the blinds are made
of wood.

Wall unit with alcove
to a Laporte design.

↖
The sitting room with furniture by
Christian Liaigre and Promemoria.
The coffee table and pouf are a design by The Office.
Oak parquet was selected for the floor.
The surround of the open fireplace is in veneer
and matt lacquer work. Built-in TV.

The parents' bedroom.
All of the cupboards
and panelling are
in carefully selected
sycamore veneer.
White leather
Christian Liaigre
footstool.
A serene atmosphere,
accentuated by the soft
beige tones.

SYMBIOSIS

Stephanie Laporte (The Office) created a contemporary interior for a young family with children in a former presbytery that is a listed building. Architect J.P. Decordier was responsible for the extension and restoration work for the project. After the structural work was completed, the work of the interior architect began. It was of prime importance to create a symbiosis between the old and new parts of the building, whilst retaining the character of the original presbytery. This constant search for the ideal balance resulted in a very special project. Contemporary art was selected for the house in collaboration with Deweer Art Gallery..

www.stephanielaporte.be

The glass wall in the entrance hall surrounds the
old plastered exterior wall.
Like the rest of the exterior walls, this was
intentionally given a rough finish in order to
emphasise that it was originally an outside wall.
Two works of art by Andy Wauman.

↗
The restoration of the
old mouldings on the
wall and ceilings was
very important here.
Works by Jan Fabre and Josef
Felix Müller create a special
atmosphere in this room.

↖
The bar and sitting area, finished in dark
materials: Colorbel, tinted glass and Corian.
The bar was completely custom-built to the
specifications of the owner of the house.
The door to the left of the bar leads to the wine
cellar.
The "floating" work of art is by Panamarenko.
Wall unit with alcove for storage space and a
work of art by Josef Felix Müller.

The office by the sitting area is
finished in dark wood throughout
with a dark carpet.
Wooden blinds on the windows and a
number of light-hearted additions: a
chair in green velvet and an African
lamp with hedgehog spines.

The kitchen, which can be closed off from the corridor with a large pivoting panel, was created in collaboration with Obumex.

A HOLIDAY ATMOSPHERE

For this home, idyllically situated in Walloon Brabant, the challenge was to
reconcile a wooden building structure with a contemporary interior.
A successful project: when you enter this home, you are overwhelmed by a true holiday feel.
Architect: Gregory Dellicour. Building contractor: Mi Casa.

www.ensembleetassocies.be   www.micasa.be   www.gregorydellicour.be

The entrance hall opens out both onto the living room (right) and the kitchen (left).

Armchairs by Christian Liaigre and a pouffe in blue natural cow leather. A weathered carpet in cow leather from Maison de Vacances.

↖
A library in sandblasted, black stained oak.

The L-shaped living room is oriented around the hearth and library wall, entirely finished in sandblasted, black stained oak. A design by Ensemble & Associés.
On one side the hearth-fire (on bio-ethanol) limits the TV-corner.

A table by
Christian Liaigre
and CH24 chairs
designed by
Hans Wegner.
Photography by
Franck Christen.

The master bedroom and its dressing rooms were realised completely in sandblasted oak. A suede pouffe from XVL.

A FLOWING CIRCULATION

When this project was entrusted to Ensemble & Associés, the property developer had just taken possession of two separate structurally finished apartments with a total surface area of 350 m². The mission was to create a single duplex with a large reception area and a flowing circulation between the spaces, all in grey-black-white shades.

www.ensembleetassocies.be

The stairs in a metal structure is covered with stained oak.

This dressing room is finished in sandblasted and stained larch.

A HOUSE NESTLED IN THE HEART
OF THE GAUME REGION

This small village home, nestled in the heart of the Gaume region,
was removed completely to house a young family.
The resolutely contemporary interior, in contrast with the authentic
character of the facades, was rethought to maximise the space.
There is a view of everything from the kitchen ... the living room, the dining
room and the family room, all designed in neutral, soft shades.
A house where it is pleasant to spend time, surrounded by beautiful nature.

www.ensembleetassocies.be

Stairs in bleached oak.

↖

The joinery was designed
by Ensemble & Associés
and realised in varnished
medium and black textile.

The main bathroom
in Crema composite
stone and sandblasted,
bleached oak.

RESTORATION OF A 19TH-CENTURY FARMHOUSE

In the green countryside of Antwerp, a couple of decorators and architects, seduced by nature and minimalism, moved into a XIXth century farmhouse. Antiquities and contemporary art converge in an atmosphere that is continuously renewed, at the cadence of their acquisitions. The owners of this place, being used at the same time as single family home and Polyèdre's headquarter, warmly welcome you twice a year. Restructuring spaces, as in this old 1895 fruit plantation, searching for quality materials, authentic furniture, items of curiosity, colours and fabrics and combining them in a contemporary ambience. Such is the challenge assigned to Henri-Charles and Natasha Hermans.

www.polyedre.be

Overview of the house and its various buildings.

Collector's items selected for the main drawing room.

View of the main building's drawing room, ambience basking in white shades, modern lighting, and furnishings of various styles.

↑

Tangled up in white, the bedroom housed under the roof, is a haven of serenity. Furniture pieces and items of various styles and eras are inviting for the journey… Bed adorned with a small oak bench, achieved at the Polyèdre work studio.

Bath room, with a rounded design bath. Toilet vanity, custom made in aged oak at the Polyèdre work studio. The shower corner and toilets are illuminated by a charming bull's-eye window.

A TIMELESS MANOIR

Within a setting of lovely park trees, Costermans Villa Projects realised a timeless English manor. The architectural design and use of materials have strong English roots. Old bricks (baked in open ovens), oak windows, recuperated roof tiles and elegant wrought ironwork melt into a harmonious and timeless whole. The garden architecture was approached in a playful way in order to respect its park-like character as much as possible. When making a stroll through the garden, you will meet a renovated pond surrounded by cobbles from the Meuse River: a closed meander of the nearby brook. When further following the path, you will cross the oak outhouse and parade onwards along some romantic cupids.

www.costermans-projecten.be

One imagines oneself to be in a magnificent hunting lodge with its rough old plank floors and subtly chosen furniture.

↑
The guestroom fully connects to the nice romantic atmosphere of the house, and has a lovely garden-view.

At the second and top floors are relax rooms with spa and billiard.

TIMELESS AUTHENTICITY AND TEMPORARY COMFORT

Paul Vanrunxt and Ludo Bruggen met each other in 1993. One was passionate about architecture, the other one about new building techniques and interior design. "Vincent Bruggen" became a fact. Shortly after this the first show country house was built. The most recent one in 2004 in Keerbergen, in the province of Flemish Brabant. Today Vincent Bruggen create about twenty personalized country-houses per year. From foundations to kitchens and built-in closets, everything is carried out by their own skilled staff. Each day about seventy zealous people are ready to put down a new reference in Canadian wood skeleton construction. Pleasant living conditions with a low energy expenditure. For the design of his own house, Paul Vanrunxt himself was inspired by old mansions with high ceilings: a symbiosis of authenticity, timelessness and temporary comfort.

www.vincentbruggen.be

The massive oak doors, also from their own workshop, reach the ceiling.

↑
The playroom of Cato and Victor. In front of the window the DCW Chair of Charles Eames.

↖
When entering the house you immediately stand centrally between the two fireplaces of the 'black' and the 'white' reception room.

A 3,5 meter high panoramic window with a view on the backyard.

A RESPECTFUL RENOVATION

This house, situated in one of the most beautiful streets in Antwerp, was seriously renovated with respect for the distinctive original architecture and for the valuable materials that were very much worth preserving. Along the outside, the existing painted windows were replaced by windows to be aged in Afrormosia hardwood, the paint on the façades was removed and replaced by softer limewash paint. At the backside, an oak pointed gable creates a warm atmosphere, the shiny black roof tiles had to make place for softer grey-brown tinted French tiles. Black shutters and gates create some chic. A well-thought out garden architecture with some formal accents at the front, further melting into more fanciful shapes with a lot of green structures.

www.costermans-projecten.be

The azure swimming pool is accompanied by a stylish oak pool house with a thatched roof. It is a nice place to stay on a warm day or at night by the open fire below this covered terrace.

AN INTIMATE AND CONTEMPORARY APARTMENT

For this apartment situated in a building from the 1980's belonging to a private domain,
the intervention of Ebony Interiors was requested to create a contemporary 'world'.
For Ebony, Mario Bruyneel created harmony and comfort using natural and top
quality materials as well as the "Ebony-Interiors Colors" palette of colours.
All the built-in furniture was also designed by him.

www.ebony-interiors.com

A sliding wall in two sections makes it possible to separate the kitchen, custom-made with a work surface in composite stone. The bench/table can be used as a breakfast corner but also as a work surface.

The customised bedroom furniture items were realised in natural oak, those of the dressing room in painted MDF in the 'Ebony-Interiors' colours and in leather.

↖
The bookcase was custom made by Ebony. It holds the TV, the loudspeakers and the remote motors for unveiling the television (in the middle of the item of furniture).

BAUHAUS INSPIRATION

This home in the German speaking part of Belgium was designed in 2007 by the architect Josef Kirschvink, who was inspired by Bauhaus. Yvonne Hennes (Project by PHYL) realised the total layout of this striking country estate with approximately 360 m2 of living space. The challenge consisted of creating both an ideal living environment and a workplace: both functions had to be combined harmoniously and still be kept separate. The left wing of the residence consists of the garage, carport and the living area. The offices of the interior architecture firm are to the right. These two wings are separated by a piece of "sliding furniture": a sliding bookcase adjoining the offices. The discrete colour palette is in perfect symbiosis with the architecture.

www.projectbyphyl.com

A table and tabouret from Maxalto (Simplice collection). The two armchairs are also from Maxalto (Apta collection). Lamps by Piet Boon, model Klaar.
Artworks by Han Lei, "Fictional Portraits".

The kitchen was realised by Obumex in oak (Cartier finish, sandblasted in Terre de Sienne). The barstools (Bataille + ibens) were also supplied by Obumex in the same wood finish. Tap by Guglielmi.
Chairs designed in leather by Piet Boon (model Siebe).
Parquet floor in brushed and grey stained oak.

↖
The table to the left of the photography is from Maxalto (Apta collection), and the sofas as well.
The round table and the small tables are also from Maxalto, but from the Simplice collection.
The two chairs on the background are by Casa Milano, "Ming".
A lamp by Gunther Lambert, "Havanna Club".

SPACE AND LIGHTNESS IN A VILLA APARTMENT

Gilles de Meulemeester (Ebony Interiors) transformed two ground floor apartments in a building designed by Marc Corbiau into a very large (c. 450 m²) apartment south of Brussels. The master of the house (a loyal customer of Ebony Interiors) asked Gilles de Meulemeester to create a single large, harmonious and warm space. He realised this by revising both the halls, the living rooms and the bedrooms completely. An identical custom-made parquet floor, grey stained oak panelling was installed throughout the entire space. Special attention was paid to the lighting: clear during the day, warm and intimate in the evening.

www.ebony-interiors.com

The TV-room with sofas and a pouffe from Liaigre, a carpet from Jules Flipo (Milleraies) and a work by Mouffe. Custom made bookcase in bleached and sandblasted oak with red painted elements. A Manhattan chair (Interni Edition).

The dressing room (also custom-made) is finished in bleached oak. Surfaces in piqué leather and a red tabouret from Promemoria. The hanging lamp was custom-made in linen. A velvet chair from Promemoria (model Bilou Bilou) in the background.

↖
The dining room is a large, open space with two sliding doors that make it possible to separate it from the kitchen. Walls painted with Pierre de Lune paints (Ebony-Colours), curtains in glazed linen. J.C. 1 wall lights in patinised metal designed by Gilles de Meulemeester. The furniture against the wall is finished in metal and buffalo skin.
Table and chairs by Interni Edition and a custom-made, hand-knotted wool and hemp rug.

FACELIFT FOR A SEASIDE APARTMENT

This seaside apartment was given a thorough facelift by interior architect Marie-France Stadsbader and was then carried out by Obumex. The circulation was revised completely, all the small spaces and numerous doors were reduced to the strictly necessary. Perspectives were created from each place to give as much sense of space as possible and also to draw in the light. The natural materials teak and Carrara marble can be found throughout the apartment but always used in a different way so that everything is in harmony.

mst@cantillana.com   www.obumex.be

The kitchen forms the division between the living room and the dining area, in which the blue glass from the kitchen can be opened up to allow contact with the dining room. In its closed state this creates a strong accent for the dining room.

↖
The niche in the living room is clad entirely in teak and serves as a reading corner.
The open fire was also custom made with a pivoting door to its right, which conceals the television. A Flexform sofa is combined with furniture by Poul Kjaerholm.

RESTORATION OF A 17TH-CENTURY CONVENT FARM

This enclosed convent farm, situated in Flemish Brabant, was built in the seventeenth century with a double wall: one around the farm buildings and one around the farmyard. The low-lying farmhouse was in a very bad state of repair. The house, consisting of two floors and seven bays, the stables and the barn, the gatehouse and the small service buildings were all restored very thoroughly and adapted by architect Bernard De Clerck. The moat was dug out, the grounds were laid out according to the old model and supplemented with new rows of trees. The canals have been deepened. Antiques and decoration: Garnier. Reclaimed materials: Rik Storms.

info@bernarddeclerck.be

The swimming pool has a sheltered position by the garden wall and the wooden "cart house".

↑
This oak construction makes outdoor dining possible. Twig chairs accentuate the rural atmosphere.

The library is
panelled throughout
in painted solid wood
panelling.

A HISTORIC TOLLHOUSE

This historic mansion in the centre of Ghent has a history that goes back to the
middle of the fifteenth century, when a tollhouse was built on this site.
Around 1867, the property was substantially rebuilt: the stepped gable
disappeared, making way for the stately mansion in its current form.
The house has undergone a process of renovation by its current
owners – a young couple with three growing children –
in close collaboration with architect Stéphane Boens.

www.stephaneboens.be

The pool house has been constructed with rough oak planks and reclaimed slates.

An interior view of the pool house, with a shower and toilet behind the curved wall.

↖
The current owners bought the next-door property, which has given magnificent proportions to this city garden. There is even space for a herb garden and a barn, built with rough oak planks and reclaimed Boom tiles, still following the designs of Stéphane Boens.

PUBLISHER
BETA-PLUS Editions
www.betaplus.com

PHOTOGRAPHY
Jo Pauwels

DESIGN
Polydem – Nathalie Binart

ISBN : 978-90-8944-112-6

Coordination production printing and binding :
www.belvedere.nl - André Kloppenberg
Printing and binding: Printer Trento, Italy